SCOTLAND'S
KINGS & QUEENS

ALAN BOLD

D0113421

Origins of the Kingdom

The kingdom of Scotland began as a tribal contest and ended as a political controversy. Prehistoric Scotland north of the Forth was dominated by the Picts, the broch-building Brythonic Celts who had come to Scotland from central Europe. In AD 83 the Romans, under Julius Agricola, defeated Pictish tribes, under Calgacus at Mons Graupius. This victory over Caledonia (as the Romans called the area to the north of Britannia) was not consolidated and 40 years later emperor Hadrian constructed a defensive wall to contain the Picts. After the Roman withdrawal of 407, Caledonia (Gaelic: Alba) was divided between four tribes, three of whom were of Celtic origin: the Picts, who ruled from Orkney to the Forth; the Scots, who controlled the Argyllshire area; the Britons, who settled in Strathclyde. The fourth group, the Angles, inhabited Lothian.

It was the Scots who were to shape the nation they gave a name to. They had come to Alba from Dalriada (Antrim) in northern Ireland and in c. 500 established a new Dalriadic dynasty. An Irish Scot, Columba, brought Christianity to Alba and his conversion of the Druidic Picts prepared the ground for the eventual Scottish absorption of Pictland. In 834 a battle between Alpin, king of the Daltriadic Scots, and Eoghann, king of the Picts, was overwhelmed by a Norse army. Both kings died and the Scoto-Pictish dispute was resolved in the person of the one man strong enough to assert his claim (through Scottish father and Pictish kinswomen) to both kingdoms.

BELOW: The Stone of Destiny, said to have been brought by Fergus Mor mac Erc to Scotland in c. 500. Kenneth MacAlpin moved it to Scone for his coronation in 843 and successive kings were crowned on it. The stone was taken to Westminster Abbey by Edward I in 1296, but was returned to Scotland in 1996.

RIGHT: A detail from the 16th-century Seton Armorial showing Robert the Bruce with his first wife, Isabella of Mar. Their daughter Marjory married Walter Stewart, and Marjory's son Robert II founded the House of Stewart.

2 Origins of the Kingdom

HOUSE OF ALPIN

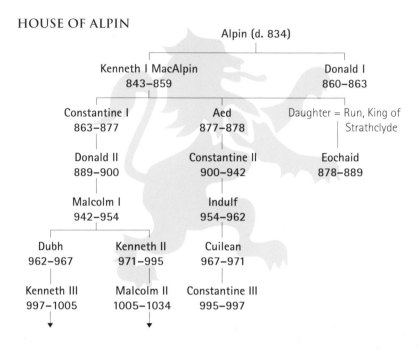

Alpin (d. 834)

- Kenneth I MacAlpin 843–859
  - Constantine I 863–877
    - Donald II 889–900
      - Malcolm I 942–954
        - Dubh 962–967
          - Kenneth III 997–1005
        - Kenneth II 971–995
          - Malcolm II 1005–1034
  - Aed 877–878
    - Constantine II 900–942
      - Indulf 954–962
        - Cuilean 967–971
          - Constantine III 995–997
  - Daughter = Run, King of Strathclyde
    - Eochaid 878–889
- Donald I 860–863

THE HOUSE OF ALPIN

Kenneth MacAlpin 843–59
In 843 Kenneth Macalpin, king of the Scots, acquired Pictland. The united Celtic kingdom was known as Scotia. Subsequently, Kenneth unsuccessfully invaded Lothian six times. He moved the centre of his kingdom from Dalraida to the Pictish east, set the ancient Stone of Destiny in Scone where he was crowned King of Scotia, and transferred St Columba's relics from Iona to Dunkeld (though in 943 King Constantine II had them taken to St Andrews).

Malcolm II 1005–34
The final king of the House of Alpin (crowned at Scone like all his predecessors) kept himself in power by a shrewd combination of tenacity and ruthlessness. In 1018 his victory at the Battle of Carham added Lothian to the kingdom of Scotia and when he failed to produce a son he cleared the royal path for his grandson Duncan by murdering the grandson of Kenneth III.

THE HOUSE OF DUNKELD

Duncan I 1034–40
Duncan (born c. 1001) was the first of the new royal House of Dunkeld and, by adding Strathclyde to his grandfather's kingdom, first monarch of a united Scotland. The hereditary right to the throne of his two sons, Malcolm Canmore and Donald Ban, was threatened by his cousin Macbeth, who claimed the kingdom on the grounds of tanistry. The matter was settled in 1040 near Elgin, when Macbeth killed Duncan in battle.

Macbeth 1040–57
Another grandson of Malcolm II, Macbeth (born c. 1005) had as good a claim to the throne as Duncan. Shakespeare's poetic licence distorted the historical facts, which show that Macbeth ruled Scotland quite successfully for 17 years and was secure in his marriage to Kenneth III's granddaughter Cruoch (who had a son, Lulach, by a previous marriage). In 1045 Macbeth defeated and killed Duncan's

ABOVE: A slab from the Antonine Wall, built by the Romans from the Forth to the Clyde, in AD 142, showing a Roman soldier on horseback subduing Picts. Yet the Romans were unable to add Caledonia to their vast empire.

RIGHT: Design from a Pictish cross-slab of the 8th century.

HOUSE OF DUNKELD

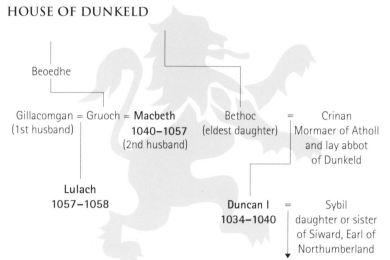

Beoedhe

Gillacomgan = Gruoch = **Macbeth**
(1st husband)   **1040–1057**
                     (2nd husband)

Bethoc = Crinan
(eldest daughter) Mormaer of Atholl
                   and lay abbot
                   of Dunkeld

Lulach
1057–1058

Duncan I = Sybil
1034–1040 daughter or sister
           of Siward, Earl of
           Northumberland

father Crinan at Dunkeld. However in 1054 he was defeated by Malcolm Canmore at Scone, and in 1057 killed by Malcolm Canmore at Lumphanan.

Lulach (the Fool) 1057–58
Lulach succeeded his stepfather, Macbeth, and after a few months of rule was killed at Strathbogie by Malcolm Canmore.

THE HOUSE OF CANMORE

Malcolm III (Canmore) 1058–93
After the defeat of his father, Duncan I, Malcolm Canmore (Gaelic *ceann Mor:* bighead or great chief), born *c.* 1031, took refuge with his uncle, Siward of Northumbria, and thus acquired Anglo-Saxon attitudes. His two acts of regicide established him as a formidable warrior-king; his first marriage produced three children of whom the eldest son, Duncan, was the heir apparent. In 1066

the Norman Conquest forced many English refugees into Lothian, among them Edgar the Atheling (Anglo-Saxon heir to the English throne) and his sister Margaret. Malcolm married Margaret in 1069 and subsequently transformed Scotland, a feat described glowingly in the Anglo-Saxon Chronicle. What Margaret actually did was persuade her illerate husband to undermine the Celtic traditions: he Romanised the Celtic Church, substituted Saxon for Gaelic as the court language and replaced the clan system with a form of feudalism. His dream of expanding his kingdom into England turned into a nightmare when William the Conqueror advanced into Scotland in 1072. At Abernethy Malcolm was forced to submit as William's man and to deliver his son Duncan to the English court as hostage. In 1093 Malcolm was ambushed and killed at Alnwick during his fifth invasion of England.

LEFT: Edinburgh Castle viewed from the north-west. Queen Margaret died here in 1093. During the Reformation, when many shrines were being destroyed, the Abbot of Dunfermline put the head of the then Saint Margaret into a jewelled case, and for safekeeping brought it to Mary Queen of Scots, who awaited the birth of her child in Edinburgh Castle.

HOUSE OF CANMORE

Malcolm III Canmore 1058–1093 = Ingibiorg daughter of Finn Arnasson, widow of Thorfinn, Jarl of Orkney (1st wife) = St Margaret (d. 1093) daughter of Edward Atheling of England (2nd wife)

Donald III Ban 1093–May 1094 and Nov 1094–1097

Duncan II May–Nov 1094 = Ethelreda daughter of Gospatrick, Earl of Northumberland

Edgar 1098–1107

Alexander I 1107–1124 = Sybilla natural daughter of Henry I

David I The Saint 1124–1153 = Matilda (d. 1131) daughter of Waltheof, Earl of Huntingdon, and widow of Simon St Lis, Earl of Northampton

Henry Earl of Huntingdon (d. 1152) = Ada daughter of William de Warenne, Earl of Surrey

Malcolm IV The Maiden 1153–1165

William I The Lion 1165–1214 = Ermengarde (d. 1234) daughter of Richard, Viscount de Beaumont

David Earl of Huntingdon = Matilda (d. 1233) daughter of hugh Keveliock, Earl of Chester

Margaret (d. 1275) daughter of Henry III, King of England (1st wife) = Alexander III 1249–1286

Alexander II 1214–1249 = Joan (d. 1238) daughter of John King of England (1st wife) = Marie daughter of Enguerand III, Baron de Coucy (2nd wife)

Margaret (d. 1283) = Erik Magnusson King of Norway 1280–1299

Margaret (The Maid of Norway) 1286–1290

ABOVE: St Margaret, Queen of Malcolm III, from a 15th-century illumination. Under her influence, life in court became more civilised and many English fashions and customs were adopted. She founded many monasteries, and for her benefactions was canonised in 1251.

ABOVE RIGHT: St Margaret's Chapel, situated at the highest part of Edinburgh Castle. It was begun by Queen Margaret and modified by her son David I. Margaret virtually secluded herself in the chapel in pursuit of her religious ideals and died there after hearing of the death of her husband and eldest son at Alnwick.

Donald Ban 1093–94

The opposition of Malcolm's younger brother, Donald Ban (Gaelic: the white), born c. 1033, to the anti-Celtic innovations made Donald popular outside Lothian and he claimed the Crown on the grounds of tanistry, only to be deposed a year later by Malcolm's son, Duncan, backed by the might of the English king William Rufus.

Duncan II May–November 1094

Born in c. 1060, Duncan, sent as a hostage to the English court in 1072, had formed a close friendship with William Rufus. But his position as virtual English vassal was unpopular in Scotland. His stepbrother, Edmund, and Donald Ban combined to defeat and kill him at Mondynes.

Donald Ban and Edmund 1094–97

After being deposed Donald Ban joined forces with his cousin Edmund (one of Malcolm and Margaret's six sons) to defeat and kill Duncan II. Together they ruled Scotland (Donald in Scotia, Edmund in Lothian and Strathclyde). They were opposed by Edmund's brother Edgar who, declaring himself a vassal of William Rufus, enlisted an English army to overthrow the royal pair. Edmund was pardoned and became a monk; Donald Ban was blinded and sentenced to life imprisonment. As a reprisal Donald strangled his nephew David's eldest son; he was buried at Dunkeld and reinterred at Iona.

Edgar (the Peaceable) 1097–1107

Edgar was the fourth son of Malcolm Canmore and Queen Margaret, born c. 1074. His submissive attitude to England, his gift of the Western Isles to king Magnus Barelegs of Norway, and his encouragement of Anglo-Norman immigrants to Scotland earned him the derisory nickname the Peaceable. He moved the royal residence from Dunfermline to Edinburgh Castle and, an unmarried man, bequeathed his kingdom to his brothers Alexander (as monarch) and David (as king's lieutenant and ruler of Lothian and Strathclyde).

had a legitimate claim to a large part of northern England. David, one of the greatest Scottish kings, was brought up at the court of Henry I and played politics by switching his support between Henry I's daughter Matilda and her cousin Stephen. On

ABOVE: *Melrose Abbey, founded by David I, in memory of his mother, Queen (later Saint) Margaret. Robert the Bruce's heart is buried here.*

Alexander I (the Fierce) 1107–24

Born c. 1077, Alexander was married to an illegitimate daughter of Henry I (who in turn married Alexander's sister Maud) but produced no legitimate offspring. He was called the Fierce after ferociously dealing with an uprising in Moray. Though technically a vassal of the English king, he stood for a Scottish identity, especially in ecclesiastical matters. He dissuaded Scottish bishops from accepting the authority of York and appointed his mother's biographer Turgot to the see of St Andrews.

David I 1124–53

The sixth and last son (born c. 1080) of Malcolm Canmore and Queen Margaret, he married a granddaughter of Earl Siward of Northumbria, and the death of Henry I he took advantage of the resultant confusion to press into England, taking Carlisle and Newcastle before he was defeated in 1138 at the Battle of the Standard near Northallerton. King Stephen was in no position to alienate the Scottish king and by the Treaty of Durham (1139) David gained control of Northumbria. His impact on Scotland was immense and he systematically transformed a Celtic society into a feudal one, he encouraged Anglo-Norman tenants; he founded royal burghs (like Stirling, Perth, Dunfermline and Edinburgh); he issued the first Scottish coinage; he honoured his mother's legendary piety by establishing monastic centres (at Melrose and Holyrood for example). As

well as imposing the rule of law on his kingdom David influenced linguistic developments, so that while Gaelic was spoken by highlanders, Inglis, a Scottish variant of English, was adopted further south. His only son Earl Henry died in 1152 and he appointed his grandson Malcolm as his successor.

Malcolm IV (the Maiden) 1153–65

A year after David's grandson (born 1142) came to the throne, Henry II became King of England and in 1157 Malcolm was forced to renounce his rights to Northumbria. In Scotland he was more successful, using his own brain and the brawn of his Anglo-Norman tenants to keep peace in the Highlands. His nickname, the Maiden, refers to his vow of chastity.

William (the Lion) 1165–1214

Born in 1143, William succeeded his unmarried brother and in 1174 invaded England, only to be ignominiously defeated and captured at Alnwick. After being imprisoned in Normandy, William was released in return for accepting Henry II as overlord of Scotland. In 1189 he bought back the sovereignty of Scotland by donating 10,000 merks to Richard I's third crusade. William's marriage produced a son, Alexander, in 1198, he foolishly paid a dowry of 15,000 merks to secure the marriage of his two daughters to King John's sons, a bargain broken by the English king.

Alexander II 1214–49

On Alexander's accession, the odious King John declared he would hunt the red fox cub from his den. Alexander reciprocated by backing the barons who made John seal the Magna Carta in 1215. By marrying John's daughter Joan, Alexander became brother-in-law of the new English king, Henry III, from whom he demanded the return of William the Lion's dowry as well as Northumbria. A diplomatic treaty of York in 1236 fixed the Border on the Tweed–Solway line. Alexander's second marriage, to Marie de Coucy, offended the English who feared a Franco-Scottish Alliance.

ınıs evene. ın loco

̃ onceffıt· Ira fah

Alexander III 1249–86

Alexander III was eight when he inherited the Scottish kingdom and 10 when he married Henry III's daughter Margaret in 1251. As boy-king he cleverly avoided the issue of England's feudal superiority, later establishing good relations with his brother-in-law Edward I. Under him Scotland, with a population of around 400,000, enjoyed a golden age of prosperity. Towns like Berwick grew rich on foreign trade, wool, fur and fish were exported; churches and castles proliferated. He dealt with the Norse threat and regained the Western Isles by defeating old king Haakon of Norway at the battle of Largs in 1263 and signing the treaty of Perth three years later. However in 1275 his wife Margaret,

and soon after their three children, died, leaving his granddaughter Margaret, Maid of Norway, as heir apparent. In the hope of producing a male heir Alexander took a second wife. Yolande, in 1285. That year he was riding to Kinghorn one stormy night to be with his new wife when his horse stumbled and threw him over a cliff to his death.

Margaret (Maid of Norway) 1286–90

The daughter of Alexander III's daughter Margaret (who died bearing her) and Erik II of Norway was three when she became Queen of Scotland in 1286. By the treaties of Salisbury (1289) and Birgham (1290), Edward I took advantage of the situation by arranging a marriage between the Maid and his son, the heir Edward. This was not to be for Margaret died (in Orkney from seasickness) on the voyage from Norway. As a macabre footnote to Margaret's brief career, in 1300 a Lubeck woman claiming to be the Maid of Norway, and thus named The False Margaret, was burned at Bergen.

The House of Canmore died with the Maid of Norway and 13 Competitors laid claim to the vacant throne. Two of them were descended from David I: John Balliol (great-grandson) and Robert Bruce (grandson). Edward I was asked to decide the issue; he first persuaded the Competitors to acknowledge him as overlord of Scotland then, at Berwick Castle, declared in favour of Balliol.

John Balliol 1292–96

After being crowned at Scone, where for the last time a Scottish king sat on the Stone of Destiny, Balliol (born c. 1250) went to Newcastle to reaffirm Edward I as his overlord. Subsequently Edward I took every opportunity to humiliate Balliol. The worm finally turned in 1295 with a treaty that initiated the 'auld alliance' with France. Edward's response was to invade Scotland the following year to crush the revolt. At Brechin, Balliol was forced to pledge Scotland to Edward I and, as a final indignity before being sent to the Tower of London, had the royal arms stripped from his tunic earning him the nickname 'Toom Tabard' (Empty Coat). Freed in 1299, he died in retirement in Normandy in 1315.

HOUSE OF BALLIOL

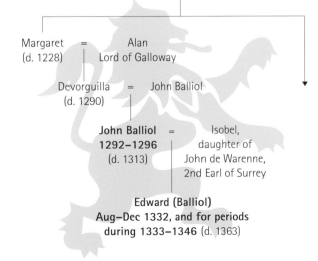

Margaret = Alan
(d. 1228) Lord of Galloway

Devorguilla = John Balliol
(d. 1290)

John Balliol = Isobel,
1292–1296 daughter of
(d. 1313) John de Warenne,
2nd Earl of Surrey

Edward (Balliol)
**Aug–Dec 1332, and for periods
during 1333–1346** (d. 1363)

ABOVE LEFT: The coronation of Alexander III at Scone, from a 15th-century manuscript.

HOUSE OF BRUCE

Isobel (d. 1251) = Robert Bruce, Lord of Annandale

Robert Bruce (d. 1295) = Isobel (d. 1254), daughter of Gilbert de Clare, 4th Earl of Gloucester

Robert Bruce (d. 1304) = Margaret, Countess of Carrick, widow of Adam de Kilconcath

Robert I (Bruce) 1306–1329 = Isobel, daughter of Donald, 6th Earl of Mar (1st wife) = Elizabeth (d. 1327), daughter of Richard de Burgh, 3rd Earl of Ulster (2nd wife)

Marjorie (d. 1316) = Walter, 6th High Steward of Scotland

David II 1329–1371 = Joan (d. 1362), daughter of Edward II, King of England (1st wife) = Margaret (div. 1370 and d. 1375), daughter of Sir Malcolm Drummond and widow of Sir John Logie (2nd wife)

Above: David II after the Battle of Neville's Cross (1346). An unworthy son to Robert the Bruce, he spent eight years as the guest of the French and 11 years as Edward III's prisoner.

After deposing John Balliol in 1296, Edward I returned to Westminster with the Stone of Destiny. He then proceeded to hammer the Scots into submission. But the ceaseless pressure rebounded with the emergence of William Wallace of Elerslie in 1297. Wallace murdered the English sheriff of Lanark, harassed the English court at Scone, won a brilliant victory at Stirling Bridge and took the title Guardian of Scotland. In 1298 Wallace was defeated by Edward at Falkirk and went underground for seven years. In 1305 he was captured near Glasgow, tried at Westminster Hall and convicted of treason. He was hanged, drawn and quartered; his piked head being displayed on London Bridge while the four bits of his body were sent to Newcastle, Berwick, Stirling and Perth in an attempt to destroy the Scottish spirit of revolt. Within a year, though, Robert the Bruce had himself crowned King of Scotland at Scone.

Robert I (the Bruce) 1306–29

Robert the Bruce, 2nd Earl of Carrick (and grandson of old Competitor Bruce) was born in Ayr in 1274. He had supported Edward I against Balliol in 1296, but when Wallace renounced the Guardianship of Scotland in 1298 Bruce and Balliol's nephew John 'Red' Comyn patriotically replaced him as joint Guardians. After a quarrel with Comyn, Bruce returned to the English fold and sheepishly obtained a pardon from Edward I in 1302. Then in 1306 Bruce, ostensibly seeking a reconciliation with Comyn, impulsively stabbed his rival in church at Dumfries. For this he was outlawed by Edward I and excommunicated by Clement V.

Rather than accept the life of a landless fugitive, Bruce claimed the Scottish throne as great-great-grandson of David I and was crowned at Scone in 1306. The task of restoring independence was made easier when in 1307 Edward I was succeeded by the ineffectual Edward II. At his first parliament of St Andrews in 1309, Bruce was fortified by declarations of loyalty; by 1314 Stirling was the only castle in English hands. An agreement made by the king's brother Edward Bruce stated that the castle would surrender if the English had not relieved it by Midsummer's Day.

Bruce, aware that this would mean a pitched battle, chose to exploit the strategic ground behind the Bannockburn. There, on 24 June 1314, his much smaller force spectacularly defeated Edward II's 20,000-strong army. Six years later, Bruce had the Declaration of Arbroath, an affirmation of Scottish independence, sent to Pope John XXII who waited four years before recognising him as the rightful King of Scotland. After the accession of Edward III in 1327, Bruce's army harassed the English until Edward was forced to acknowledge his sovereignty. With the war officially over by the 1328 Treaty of Northampton, Bruce, by now a dying man, asked his friend Sir James

Douglas to take his heart to the Holy Land when his body was buried in Dunfermline Abbey. But Douglas was killed in Spain and the heart was returned to Scotland to be buried in Melrose Abbey.

David II 1329–71

The son of Robert the Bruce and his second wife, Elizabeth, was diplomatically married at the age of four to Edward II's daughter Joan and became Scotland's first anointed king a year later. Resentful of the treaty of Northampton, Edward III was delighted when his vassal Edward Balliol (son of Toom Tabard) defeated David's army near Perth in 1332. Balliol was crowned at Scone but quickly ejected from Scotland by forces loyal to David II. A year later, though, he was back to defeat the Scots near Berwick. David fled to France and the Scots, under Robert the Bruce's grandson Robert Stewart, rallied a second time. In 1346, five years after returning to Scotland, David invaded England on behalf of his French friends. He was captured near Durham and in captivity became friendly with Edward III. When he returned to Scotland in 1357 on a ransom of 100,000 merks, he decided to produce an alternative heir to Robert Stewart who had been Guardian of Scotland in his absence. After Queen Joan died in 1362, he married his mistress Margaret Drummond and, when she failed to deliver an heir, attempted unsuccessfully to divorce her.

LEFT: The statue of Robert the Bruce at Bannockburn near Stirling where he routed Edward II's forces. Outnumbered three to one with only a handful of cavalry and no archers, he chose higher ground than the English, forcing them to flounder in the marsh below.

RIGHT: A portrait of James. He was nominal founder and great benefactor of St Andrew's University. His vigorous reforms made him many enemies, and he was assassinated at Perth in 1437.

TOP: James I with his Parliament shortly after his return to Scotland in 1424, after spending 18 years as the prisoner of the English. Nicknamed 'The Lawgiver', he acted strongly to restore order in the face of rebellious nobles, chaotic administration, widespread poverty and disease.

ABOVE: A portrait of James II. His coronation at Holyrood Abbey rather than Scone ended a tradition initiated by Kenneth MacAlpin in 843.

Robert II 1371–90

The surname of Stewart came from the hereditary title of an ancestor. Walter, appointed High Steward of Scotland by David I. Robert the Bruce's daughter Marjory married Walter Stewart (6th High Steward of Scotland) and died giving birth to Robert, founder of the Stewart dynasty in 1316. When be became king at the age of 54, Robert II was an experienced though diffident, man who had served as Guardian of Scotland during the enforced absence of David II. He produced 21 children (13 legitimate and eight illegitimate). In 1384 weary old Robert decreed that his eldest legitimate son should rule on his behalf.

Robert III 1390–1406

Robert III (born 1327) became king with two disadvantages: a kick from a horse had disabled him and his own name, John, had so many defeatist connotations that he assumed the title Robert III. Unable to command respect, Robert III told his queen that he was the worst of kings and the most miserable of men. He was overshadowed by his forceful brother Robert, Duke of Albany, who may have been responsible for the death of Robert III's son David. To protect his second son from Albany, Robert III sent the future James I from Scotland. When Robert died, Albany became Governor of Scotland while James I was an English prisoner. As such, Albany ruled Scotland until his death in 1420 when he was succeeded as Governor by his incompetent son Murdoch.

James I 1406–37

In 1405 Robert III's 11-year-old second son, James, had been captured by English pirates en route to France. For the next 18 years he was a prisoner of the English, though on the death of Robert III in 1406 he was recognised as James I by the Scottish parliament. In 1424 he was released on a ransom of 60,000 merks. He gradually restored respect for the monarchy and founded what was to become the Court of Session. However, conspirators who hoped to win the throne for Walter, a son of Robert II's second marriage, murdered James I at Perth where he is buried.

James II 1437–60

The six-year-old son of James I was crowned in Holyrood Abbey, Edinburgh, in 1437 and thus ended a tradition that had endured at Scone since Kenneth MacAlpin. During the minority of James

of the Fiery Face (as he was known because of a large birthmark). Scotland was ruled by two rivals: Chancellor Sir William Crichton, keeper of Edinburgh Castle, and Governor Sir Alexander Livingstone, keeper of Stirling Castle. Their fear of a Douglas coup was removed when they invited William, 6th Earl of Douglas (a great-grandson of Robert III) and his brother to the Great Hall of Edinburgh Castle where they were murdered, in the presence of James II, at the infamous Black Dinner of 1440. Twelve years later the king himself stabbed William, 8th Earl of Douglas, and later defeated the Douglases at Arkinholm. In 1460, while supporting Henry VI in the Wars of the Roses, James II was killed at the siege of Roxburgh Castle when a cannon he was supervising exploded.

HOUSE OF STEWART

Robert II = Elizabeth = Euphemia
1371–1390 (d. 1355) (d. 1387)
daughter of daughter of Hugh,
Sir Adam Mure Earl of Ross
of Rowallan (2nd wife)
(1st wife)

Robert III = Annabella   Lady Jean = 1st Sir John Keith = 2ndly, Sir John Lyon = 3rdly, Sir James
1390–1406 (d. 1401)   of Glamis   Sandilands
daughter of
Sir John Drummond

Ancestors of
H.M. Queen Elizabeth,
The Queen Mother

James I = Joan
1406–1437 (d. 1445)
daughter of
John Beaufort,
Earl of Somerset,
grandson of Edward III
(1st wife)

James IV = Margaret
1488–1513 (d. 1541)
daughter of Henry VII,
King of England

James V = Madeleine = Mary of Lorraine
1513–1542 (d. 1537) (d. 1560)
daughter of Francis I, daughter of Claude,
King of France Duke of Guise
(1st wife) (2nd wife)

James II = Marie
1437–1460 (d. 1463)
daughter of Arnold,
Duke of Gueldres

James III = Margaret   **Mary, Queen of Scots** = Francis II = 2ndly Henry Stuart = 3rdly James Hepburn
1460–1488 daughter of Christian I, **1542–1567** King of France Lord Darnley, 4th Earl of Bothwell
(assassinated) King of Denmark (deposed 1567) 1559–1560 King Consort (cr. Duke of Orkney
(d. 1486) (executed 1587) (cr. Duke of Albany 1567)
1565) (d. 1578)
(murdered 1567)

James VI = Anne
1567–1625 (d. 1619)
became James I, daughter of Frederick II
King of England King of Denmark
1603–1625

James III 1460–88

Like his father, James III (born 1451) was a minor when he succeeded to the throne after a coronation at Kelso Abbey. His mother Marie of Gueldres ruled as Regent until her death in 1463. James III's government solved the external threat by signing a truce with Edward IV, the internal problems were more intractable. On Regent Marie's death the powerful Boyd family coerced James into recognising them as his advisers but after his marriage to Margaret of Denmark in 1469, for which her father pledged Orkney and Shetland as a surrogate dowry, the king was strong enough to destroy the Boyds. A more serious challenge came from the king's brothers Alexander, Duke of Albany, and John, Earl of Mar, who were arrested in 1479 on suspicion of conspiring against the Crown. Mar died suspiciously while Albany made a spectacular escape from Edinburgh Castle and reached England where Edward IV recognised him as vassal king Alexander IV in 1482. When Albany invaded Scotland some Scottish lords hanged James III's boyfriend Robert Cochrane and imprisoned the king in Edinburgh Castle for three months

> Dool for the order sent our lads to the Border,
> The English for ance by guile wan the day;
> The Flowers of the Forest that fought aye the foremost,
> The prime of our land lie cauld in the clay.
> **JEAN ELLIOT: THE FLOWERS OF THE FOREST
> (ON JAMES IV'S DEFEAT AT FLODDEN)**

home. Scotland, under James IV, was progressive. A third university was founded at Aberdeen, the printing-press came to Scotland, architecture flourished, and an organised navy was established. But the reign ended tragically; by the 'auld alliance' James IV was bound to support France so when Henry VIII invaded France, the Scottish king invaded England. He and his army were wiped out at Flodden, on 9 September 1513.

James III tried to settle his differences with his brother but Albany again attempted to win the kingdom and was exiled to France. A third and devastating challenge to the throne emerged when Scottish lords, appalled when James III's bisexuality persuaded him to confer an earldom on his new boyfriend, John Ramsay, rallied behind the reluctant 15-year-old prince James. Father and son met at Sauchieburn near Stirling, and James III lost the battle and his life. He was buried in Cambuskenneth Abbey.

James IV 1488–1513

James IV (born 1473), distressed at his unwilling participation in the death of his father, wore an iron chain round his waist as a lifelong penance. He had all the traditional kingly qualities and presided over a glittering court. James IV recognised Perkin Warbeck as Richard IV and made a token invasion of England on behalf of the Yorkist pretender to Henry VII's throne. In 1503 James IV married Henry's daughter Margaret Tudor, in the interests of political, rather than domestic, peace for his queen was unhappy away from her

James V 1513–42

James IV's son was a little over a year old when crowned at Stirling. The leading Scottish nobles offered the Governorship to John Stuart, Duke of Albany, who was vigorously opposed by the king's mother Margaret Tudor and her second husband Archibald Douglas, 6th Earl of Angus. Albany left Scotland in 1524 and the following year Angus took control. James V endured his stepfather's oppression until 1528 when he escaped and hounded Angus out of Scotland. As a ruler, James V combined suspicion of the nobility with sympathy for his poorer subjects, among whom he travelled incognito as the 'Gudeman o'Ballengeich'. He proved a generous patron of the Catholic Church at a time of incipient Reformation, and encouraged satirical writers. He twice married Frenchwomen and supported France against Henry VIII's England. Protestant England and Catholic Scotland fought at the battle of Solway Moss in 1542. News of his army's defeat destroyed the Scottish king. A week before his death his daughter, Mary, had been born. The king prophesied 'It came with a lass, it will pass with a lass.'

ABOVE: James IV was established as an outstanding king before his hopes were crushed on the battlefield of Flodden, when the English army under the Earl of Surrey gained their greatest military victory over the Scots.

ABOVE CENTRE: James V and his second wife, Mary of Guise. His policies alienated the Scottish nobility and endeared him to the Scottish people. He died in despair after the defeat at Solway Moss in 1542. Mary was mother of Mary Queen of Scots. She became Regent in 1554 but was defeated by Protestant forces and died in Edinburgh Castle.

FAR LEFT: Hugo van der Goes' Trinity College altarpiece of 1476 shows James III (who commissioned the picture) being attended by St Andrew, patron saint of Scotland. The third figure is possibly James III's eldest son, the future James IV.

ABOVE: A portrait of Mary Queen of Scots by Francois Clouet. A widow in her teens and no longer Queen of France, she returned to Scotland in 1561 to claim her inheritance. Beautiful, high spirited, highly sexed, impulsive and a devout Roman Catholic, her arrival in a Scotland dominated by an austere Kirk was bound to cause trouble.

Mary was nine months old when crowned at Stirling Castle in 1543. She was not only Scottish queen but, as Margaret Tudor's granddaughter, next in line to the English throne after the children of Henry VIII. By the treaties of Greenwich (1543), Regent Arran arranged for Mary to marry Henry VIII's son Edward. Catholics opposed to the plan took the royal infant to Stirling Castle. Henry VIII began his rough wooing of Mary by invading Scotland in 1544 and 1545, and death too frequently intervened in the international intrigue surrounding Mary. Sent to France as a child, she married the dauphin Francois, son of Henri II, in 1558. A few months after this 'Bloody Mary' Tudor died childless and the English throne passed to her unmarried half-sister Elizabeth.

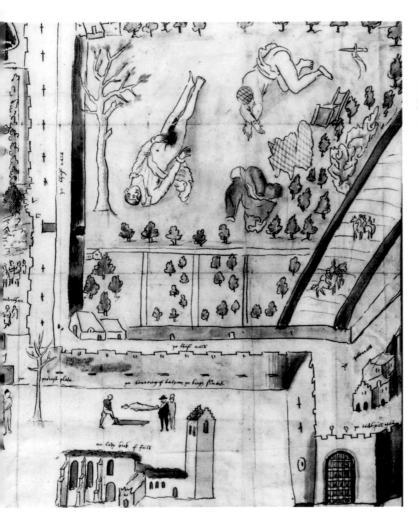

ABOVE: One of the Oxburghe Panels: three pieces embroidered by Mary Queen of Scots during her 19 years of house arrest, which were ended by her execution at Fotheringhay Castle, Northants.

LEFT: A contemporary sketch described the murder of Darnley at Kirk o'Field in 1567. Left centre, the house in which Darnley had been staying, reduced to rubble. Top right, Darnley and his page lie naked after the explosion. Below, the funeral procession. Top left, the infant James VI, Darnley's son. The cause of Darnley's death was found to have been strangulation.

BELOW LEFT: The Darnley Jewel, made in the 1570s for Margaret, Countess of Lennox, in memory of her son, Darnley, and his father Lord Lennox. Darnly was 19, four years Mary's junior, not very intelligent and notoriously vain and irresponsible. His father was killed at Stirling while acting as Regent for James VI.

From the Catholic point of view Mary had a better claim, and Henri II declared his daughter-in-law rightful Queen of England. Henri II died in 1559 and the following year both Mary's mother and husband died. She decided to return to Scotland, which, in her absence, had been transformed by John Knox into a firmly Protestant country. On her arrival in 1561 Mary immediately fell foul of Knox and the weather. She was isolated in Scotland and in 1565 married her cousin Henry Stuart, Lord Darnley, who soon demonstrated his ignoble qualities by having her secretary, David Riccio, dragged from her presence and murdered in Holyroodhouse. At the time, Mary was carrying the child James who was born in 1566. Darnley, now dispensable, was killed soon after escaping from an explosion that destroyed the house where he was staying. The probable murderer was James Hepburn, Earl of Bothwell, whom Mary married three months later. This third marriage was a personal and political tragedy for Mary. She was seized by the Protestant army at Carberry Hill, taken to Lochleven Castle where she miscarried Bothwell's twins and was forced to abdicate. She then dramatically escaped to England where her cousin Elizabeth I put her under house arrest for the remaining 19 years of her life. During her English captivity Mary encouraged attempts to release her, but for her involvement in the Babington Plot to assassinate Elizabeth I she was beheaded at Fotheringhay Castle in 1587.

James, the son of Mary Queen of Scots, was born in Edinburgh Castle on 19 June 1566 and crowned, according to Protestant rites in Holy Rude church, Stirling the following year. He was tutored by the great Latinist George Buchanan (who attempted to instil in him a hatred of his Catholic mother) and advised by four successive regents (Moray, Lennox, Mar and Morton). Passionately fond of his cousin Esme Stuart d'Aubigny, James VI was distraught when in 1582 William Ruthven, Earl of Gowrie, seized the king and expelled the cousin (who died in France a year later). After ten months of captivity James VI escaped and began his reign in earnest by making friendly overtures to his

ABOVE: James VI and I in whose person the Crowns of Scotland and England were united in 1603. With his mother a prisoner, he was brought up by a harsh tutor and subject to a tug-of-war between Catholics and Protestants. He escaped from captivity in 1583, to seize the reins of power from his Protestant kidnappers. The portrait is attributed to John de Critz.

LEFT: James VI and his mother, Mary Queen of Scots. This portrait could not have been painted from life. Mary was forced to abdicate in favour of the one-year-old James in 1567, and was a captive of Queen Elizabeth I at the time when James was the age he appears to be in the picture.

mother's captor Elizabeth I. Although he rejected Buchanan's portrayal of Mary as evil incarnate, he did nothing to secure her release and reacted to the news of her execution with a formal note of protest. In 1589 James married Anne of Denmark (by whom he had seven children, including the future Charles I) and king and queen patiently awaited the call from England. Meanwhile, James asserted his belief in the Divine Right of Kings and the right of his bishops to run the Scottish Kirk. When the Calvinist Andrew Melville protested against this policy, James VI tersely replied 'No Bishop, No King'. Then, in 1603, Elizabeth I

died and James VI's greatest wish was granted when he was crowned King of England at Westminster. The man Henri IV of France called the wisest fool in Christendom was now in control of the kingdom he called Great Britain. Both James and Anne enjoyed the move from Scotland to England. James relished the pomp and ceremony of the English court after the relative austerity of its Scottish counterpart. Anne became a patron of the architect Inigo Jones. He returned to Scotland only once in 1617, when he failed to force episcopacy on the Kirk. He died in 1625 with his reputation tarnished in England but still bright in Scotland.

ABOVE: James I of England sits in Parliament. He loved the new life in England that opened out for him in 1603, relishing the ceremony, the flattery and the luxury of the English Court. He liked the English approach to things and enjoyed the ritual of the Church of England.

As James VI's parents had both used the French spelling of their surname, the last Stewart king of Scotland became the first Stuart king of Great Britain and thus the House of Stuart was founded. Henceforth, Scotland's role in royal affairs was peripheral. Charles I's Scottish coronation took place at Holyroodhouse in 1633 and, during the English Commonweath, Charles II was proclaimed king in Edinburgh in 1649 and crowned at Scone in 1651. When Charles II's brother James II was deposed, Scottish Catholics under Viscount Dundee fought for him at the Battle of Killiecrankie in 1689, a battle Dundee died in winning. James II's son James Francis Edward Stuart, the Old Pretender, found enough support in Scotland to launch three Jacobite rebellions there: in 1708 when he was dismissed in the Firth of Forth; in 1715 when his forces fell at Sheriffmuir; and in 1719 when the Jacobites were defeated at Glenshiel. While the fortunes of James VIII and III (as he was known in France and

Jacobite Scotland) faltered, the House of Hanover (George I was a great-grandson of James VI and I) became solidly established in Britain. However, against seemingly impossible odds, the Old Pretender's son Charles Edward Stuart came to Scotland in August 1745 and, with the devoted support

of the Scottish clans, proclaimed his father King and himself Regent. By 4 December Bonnie Prince Charlie had reached Derby and George II was ready to return to Hanover. At this point, the Jacobites decided to retreat, despite the advice of their prince, and their hopes were destroyed along with the Scottish clans on the battlefield of Culloden on 16 April 1746. Bonnie Prince Charlie passed into history as a pathetic old man with a brilliant future behind him. On the death of his father in 1766 he became, for Jacobites, Charles III and even married at the age of 52 in vain hope of producing a male heir for his imaginary kingdom. When he died in 1788 his brother Cardinal York assumed the title Henry IX but, after financial ruin, eventually accepted an annual pension from George III whom he gratefully acknowledged, at his death in 1807, true successor of the Stuarts.

ABOVE: A portrait of Bonnie Prince Charlie by John Pettie. The portrait hangs in the Palace of Holyroodhouse where the Young Pretender stayed in the early days of the rising.

FACING PAGE: Combat at Culloden, 16 April 1746, when the Highlanders were defeated by Government troops, painted by David Morier for the victorious Duke of Cumberland.

LEFT: The Old Pretender in 1708. The putative James VIII and III made three unsuccessful attempts to gain the Crown.